NOV 2 8 2012

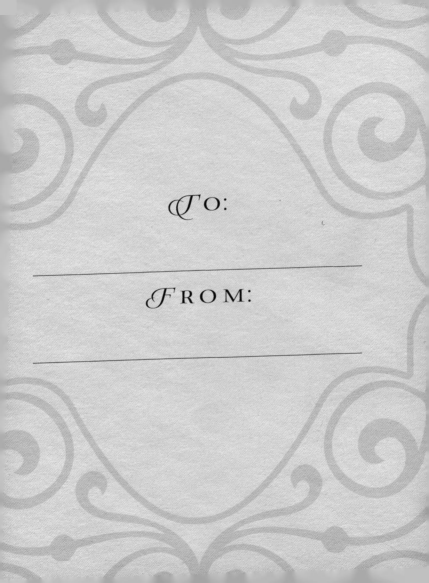

To:

_____

From:

_____

© 2012 by Richard Brunstetter and Wanda E. Brunstetter

Print ISBN 978-1-62029-137-5

Scripture quotations are taken from the King James Version of the Bible.

Cover image © Richard Brunstetter

Published by Barbour Publishing, Inc., P.O. Box 719, Uhrichsville, Ohio 44683, www.barbourbooks.com

Our mission is to publish and distribute inspirational products offering exceptional value and biblical encouragement to the masses.

Member of the
Evangelical Christian
Publishers Association

Printed in China.

A PORTRAIT of AMISH LIFE

Featuring the photography of
RICHARD BRUNSTETTER
with inspiration from **WANDA E. BRUNSTETTER,**
bestselling author of Amish fiction

BARBOUR
PUBLISHING

*A man's life consisteth not in the abundance
of things which he possesseth.*

LUKE 12:15

*R*ichard Brunstetter has had a love and respect for the Plain People since he was a boy, growing up in a Mennonite church in Pennsylvania. He has established a close friendship with many Amish people in several communities throughout America. Richard's beautiful photographs capture the simplicity of the Amish, who choose their conservative way of life over modern conveniences. The stunning photos in this book of scenic settings in many Amish communities around the country give an accurate portrayal and closer look at the Plain People's way of life, depicting their work, Christian principles, family life, and social events. You'll be fascinated with this up close view of the Amish and inspired by scripture selections and thoughts from Richard's wife, Wanda E. Brunstetter, bestselling author of Amish fiction.

Teach me thy way, O LORD,
and lead me in a plain path.

PSALM 27:11

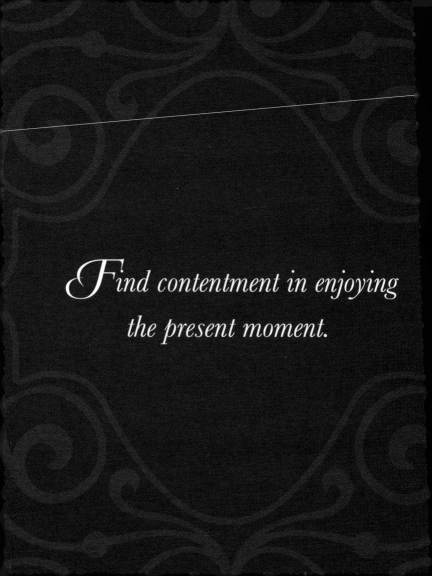

Find contentment in enjoying the present moment.

Not that I speak in respect of want: for I have learned, in whatsoever state I am, therewith to be content.

PHILIPPIANS 4:11

*The things I can see
help me trust God for the things
I cannot see.*

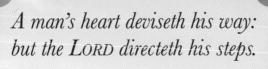

A man's heart deviseth his way:
but the LORD directeth his steps.

PSALM 27:11

*Keep looking up,
for God is looking down.*

In thee, O LORD,
do I put my trust.

PSALM 71:1

*Life with Christ is
an endless hope.*

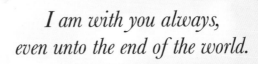

I am with you always,
even unto the end of the world.

MATTHEW 28:20

Every sunrise is a new message from God, and every sunset His signature.

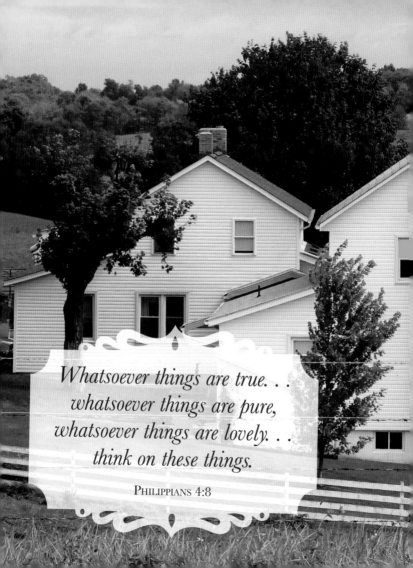

Whatsoever things are true. . . whatsoever things are pure, whatsoever things are lovely. . . think on these things.

PHILIPPIANS 4:8

God is only a prayer away.

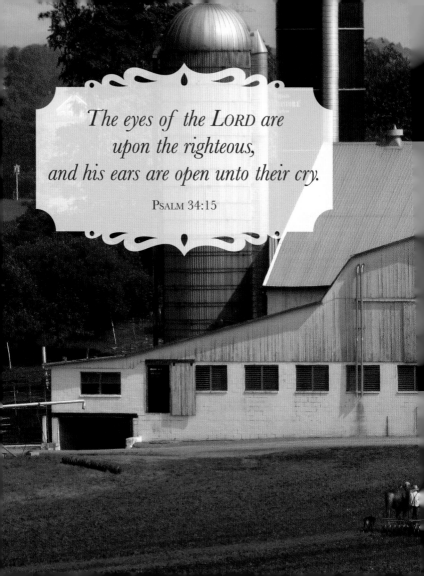

The eyes of the LORD are
upon the righteous,
and his ears are open unto their cry.

PSALM 34:15

*D*on't overlook life's
small joys while looking
for the big ones.

God that made the world and all things therein, seeing that he is Lord of heaven and earth.

ACTS 17:24

When we have nothing
left but God, we will find
that He is enough.

I will not leave you comfortless:
I will come to you.

JOHN 14:18